Dear Parents and Educators,

Welcome to Penguin Young Readers! As parents and educators, you know that each child develops at his or her own pace—in terms of speech, critical thinking, and, of course, reading. Penguin Young Readers recognizes this fact. As a result, each Penguin Young Readers book is assigned a traditional easy-to-read level (1–4) as well as a Guided Reading Level (A–P). Both of these systems will help you choose the right book for your child. Please refer to the back of each book for specific leveling information. Penguin Young Readers features esteemed authors and illustrators, stories about favorite characters, fascinating nonfiction, and more!

Apples and How They Grow

LEVEL 2

GUIDED READING LEVEL **I**

This book is perfect for a **Progressing Reader** who:
- can figure out unknown words by using picture and context clues;
- can recognize beginning, middle, and ending sounds;
- can make and confirm predictions about what will happen in the text; and
- can distinguish between fiction and nonfiction.

Here are some **activities** you can do during and after reading this book:
- Sight Words: Sight words are frequently used words that readers must know just by looking at them. These words are known instantly, on sight. Knowing these words helps children develop into efficient readers. As you read the story, point out the sight words below.

a	are	is	of
and	do	it	they

- The author writes about a "trick" apple growers use to get a tree to produce Rome apples. On a separate sheet of paper, write down the steps of the trick. Then discuss them. Also discuss what happens to make an apple blossom into an apple.

Remember, sharing the love of reading with a child is the best gift you can give!

—Bonnie Bader, EdM
  Penguin Young Readers program

*Penguin Young Readers are leveled by independent reviewers applying the standards developed by Irene Fountas and Gay Su Pinnell in *Matching Books to Readers: Using Leveled Books in Guided Reading*, Heinemann, 1999.

For Nonna and Nonno—LD

To Murphy, my favorite first-grader—TS

Penguin Young Readers
Published by the Penguin Group
Penguin Group (USA) Inc., 375 Hudson Street, New York, New York 10014, USA
Penguin Group (Canada), 90 Eglinton Avenue East, Suite 700, Toronto, Ontario M4P 2Y3, Canada
(a division of Pearson Penguin Canada Inc.)
Penguin Books Ltd., 80 Strand, London WC2R 0RL, England
Penguin Group Ireland, 25 St. Stephen's Green, Dublin 2, Ireland (a division of Penguin Books Ltd.)
Penguin Group (Australia), 250 Camberwell Road, Camberwell, Victoria 3124, Australia
(a division of Pearson Australia Group Pty. Ltd.)
Penguin Books India Pvt. Ltd., 11 Community Centre, Panchsheel Park, New Delhi—110 017, India
Penguin Group (NZ), 67 Apollo Drive, Rosedale, Auckland 0632, New Zealand
(a division of Pearson New Zealand Ltd.)
Penguin Books (South Africa) (Pty.) Ltd., 24 Sturdee Avenue,
Rosebank, Johannesburg 2196, South Africa

Penguin Books Ltd., Registered Offices: 80 Strand, London WC2R 0RL, England

Text copyright © 2003 by Laura Driscoll. Illustrations copyright © 2003 by Tammy Smith. All rights
reserved. First published in 2003 by Grosset & Dunlap, an imprint of Penguin Group (USA) Inc.
Published in 2012 by Penguin Young Readers, an imprint of Penguin Group (USA) Inc.,
345 Hudson Street, New York, New York 10014. Manufactured in China.

Library of Congress Control Number: 2003014766

ISBN 978-0-448-43275-5   10 9 8 7 6 5 4

PENGUIN YOUNG READERS

LEVEL
2
PROGRESSING
READER

Apples
and How They Grow

by Laura Driscoll
illustrated by Tammy Smith

Penguin Young Readers
An Imprint of Penguin Group (USA) Inc.

Lift, twist, pluck.

Ta-da!

It's a yummy apple!

It is fall—
apple-picking
time.

Red
Delicious

6

There are red apples, green apples, and yellow apples. There are sweet apples. There are tart apples. There are hundreds of kinds of apples!

McIntosh

Where do they come from?

Apples grow on trees.

Right?

Right.

And apple trees grow

from apple seeds.

Right?

Well, yes.

But apple seeds

can play tricks.

Take a seed from a Rome apple.

Plant it.

A tree will grow.

After many years,

it will have apples.

But they may not

be Rome apples.

You may get a tree

with sour apples . . .

. . . or an apple tree with *no* apples!

But apple growers

have tricks, too.

What is the apple grower

going to do?

He is looking for a

tree with Rome apples.

He cuts

a branch

from the tree.

He finds a
baby apple
tree.

He joins the
branch to it.

It looks
like this.

Rome
branch

Soon the two parts

grow into one tree.

Now it is a Rome tree!

The new tree

has no apples yet.

For a few years,

it just grows . . .

and grows . . .

and grows.

Then in spring,
something appears
on the branches.
Apples?

No.

Flowers!

They are called

apple blossoms

(say: BLAH-sums).

During the summer,

the flowers change.

The petals drop off.

The base of the

flower gets bigger.

Something is growing.

It is growing rounder . . .

and redder.

It is an apple—

a Rome apple!

Lift, twist, pluck . . .

. . . *crunch!*

It's yummy!